Presented to:

_____

From:

_____

Date:

_____

TRUTH AND GRACE MEMORY BOOK

BOOK 3

Ages Fourteen to Seventeen

THOMAS K. ASCOL, EDITOR

©2017 Founders Press
P.O. Box 150931
Cape Coral, FL 33915
Phone (239) 772-1400
http://www.founders.org

ISBN: 978-1-943539-07-9

Cover Design by Joshua Noom

TABLE OF
CONTENTS

66

He established a testimony in Jacob
and appointed a law in Israel,
which he commanded our fathers
to teach to their children,
that the next generation might know them,
the children yet unborn,
and arise and tell them to their children,
so that they should set their hope in God
and not forget the works of God,
but keep his commandments.

99

PSALMS 78:5-7

To
Donna,
our children,
our grandchildren,
and children yet unborn

66

Give your children big truths they can grow
into rather than light explanations they will
grow out of.

99

TEDD TRIPP

66

I learned more about Christianity from my
mother than from all the theologians in England.

99

JOHN WESLEY

INTRODUCTION

Dr. Thomas K. Ascol

Psalm 78 casts a multi-generational vision for the people of God. Asaph declares his intention to pass on to his children that which he and his generation learned from their fathers. By doing so, his children, in turn, can teach their children. "He established a testimony in Jacob and appointed a law in Israel, which he commanded our fathers to teach to their children, that the next generation might know them, the children yet unborn, and arise and tell them to their children" (Psalm 78:5-6).

The Bible teaches that children are "a heritage from the Lord" and that "the fruit of the womb is His reward" (Psalm 127:3). Each child is a gift from God. This makes parents stewards of God, entrusted with one (or more) of His greatest blessings. It also means that those who work with children are involved in a high calling.

The Truth and Grace Memory Books (*TAG* books) are designed to help parents, churches and children's workers as they fulfill that calling. Three primary ingredients are found in each book.

First and foremost is the Word of God. Several passages have been carefully selected for memorization. All Scripture throughout the Scripture Memory section is in the English Standard Version. Key Bible verses as well as longer portions are designed to introduce children to the overall scope and purpose of God's creative, providential and redemptive activity. The student who completes all three books will memorize (among other texts) the Ten Commandments, the Beatitudes, the Lord's prayer, 1 Corinthians 13, various Psalms (including 119!), plus all the books of the Bible.

Why place such an emphasis on memorizing Scripture? Listen to the Psalmist's answer: "I have stored up your word in my heart that I might not sin against You" (Psalm 119:11). Furthermore, consider the great promise God makes in Isaiah 55:10–11: "For as the rain and the snow come down from heaven, and do not return there but water the earth, making it bring forth and sprout, giving seed to the sower and bread to the eater, so shall my word be that goes out from my mouth; it shall not return to me empty, but it shall accomplish that which I purpose, and shall succeed in the thing for which I sent it." God's Spirit uses the Scripture to speak to adults and children of all ages, calling them to faith in Christ and directing in the paths of real discipleship. Therefore, as a parent who prays for the salvation and spiritual growth of your child, you must be diligent in teaching him or her the Word of God.

A second element in the workbook is a selection of sound Christian hymns to be learned and memorized. Many of these are familiar (such as the Doxology) and can be learned by very small children. Others are not so well-known but are profound in their communication of biblical truth. In all, more than 2 dozen great hymns of the faith are included.

A WORD ABOUT CATECHISMS

The third, and perhaps least familiar, ingredient are catechisms. A good catechism is a very effective tool in the hands of a dedicated parent or teacher. Each *TAG* book is built around a trustworthy, Baptist catechism. That term —"Baptist catechism"—may sound strange to many modern Baptists. They may think, as I did early in my life, that "catechism" is a Roman Catholic, Lutheran or, at best, Presbyterian word.

Of course, that simply is not true. "Catechize" is anglicized version of the Greek word, *katekeo*, which simply means "to teach." It appears, in various forms, several times in the Greek New Testament (it is translated as "taught" in Luke 1:4 and Acts 18:25).

Anyone, then, who has been taught has in some sense been catechized. But the word came to refer to a specific type of instruction early in church history. New Christians were taught the essentials of the faith by learning how to answer specific questions, which were eventually grouped together and came to be referred to simply as a "catechism."

Tom Nettles has called the 16th-century Protestant Reformation the "golden age" of catechisms. In 1562 what is arguably the most influential one of all was published as the Heidelberg Catechism. Leading reformers, most notably Martin Luther and John Calvin, produced catechisms to teach both the essentials and distinctives of their faith. In the next century, the first modern Baptists followed suit.

Early Baptist leaders regarded catechetical instruction as a valuable method to teach both children and adults the doctrinal content of the Bible. Keach's Catechism (whose author, Benjamin Keach—a 17th-century English Baptist— modeled it after the Shorter Catechism of the Westminster Assembly) was widely used among Baptists in both England and America. Charles Spurgeon (19th-century English Baptist leader) revised it slightly and reissued it for use in the Metropolitan Tabernacle.

Early Southern Baptists freely employed catechisms. One of the first publications which the Sunday School Board produced was a catechism by James Boyce, founder and first President of Southern Seminary. John Broadus also wrote a catechism which was published by the board in the 19th century. Lottie Moon used a catechism in her missionary work in China.

The *TAG* Books stand firmly in this stream of Orthodox, Protestant and Baptist catechetical instruction. Each of the three books is based on a specific catechism. *The Baptist Catechism* is reproduced in the second book, and we use this original version of the catechism so that it matches *The Baptist Catechism* set to music (which can be purchased from Founders Ministries). A simpler, more elementary one, *A Catechism for Boys and Girls*, is used in the first and *The Heidelberg Catechism for Baptists* (which draws on *The Orthodox Catechism* of 1680) is used in the third.

A WORD TO PARENTS

Raising children in the 21st century is challenging, to say the least. The temptation on parents to merely get by is great. Sometimes moms and dads simply want to make it through with the fewest possible conflicts. When this attitude is adopted parents become passive and children learn to be manipulative and the result is that neither parents nor children are happy. Though tragic, it is sadly not uncommon to see Christian homes where parents have defaulted on the responsibilities that God has entrusted to them.

Teaching their children the Word of God is at the forefront of responsibilities for Christian parents. God specifically calls Christian parents to raise their children "in the discipline and instruction of the Lord" (Ephesians 6:4). You cannot be passive and fulfill this responsibility to "bring them up" in the proper way. Prayer, discipline, godly example, and consistent, continuous, clear instruction are required.

The comprehensive nature of this responsibility is spelled out in Deuteronomy 6:4–6.

> "Hear, O Israel: The LORD our God, the LORD is one. You shall love the LORD your God with all your heart and with all your soul and with all your might. And these words that I command you today shall be on your heart. You shall teach them diligently to your children, and shall talk of them when you sit in your house, and when you walk by the way, and when you lie down, and when you rise."

In the face of such a daunting responsibility I cannot overstate the value of a well-constructed catechism to help parents in this work. By learning such a catechism a child (or adult for that matter) will be introduced to the overall biblical scheme of salvation. Such discipline will frame the mind for receiving and understanding every part of the Bible. A good catechism trains a person to read the Bible theologically.

God places the responsibility for raising children squarely on the shoulders of their parents. It is not primarily the job of church leaders or the pastor. If you are a parent then recognizing and accepting this responsibility is one of the most important things you can do. If you do not invest your time and effort to teach your children about God, be assured someone else will. Your children will be discipled by someone. They may get their ideas about God primarily from television, music or social media. If so, then they are likely to be taught that God, if He exists at all, is an irrelevant, indulgent being that is little more than a nice, kindly old man. If you do not teach your children truth and righteousness, be assured that there are a multitude of teachers in this world who would deceive them into thinking that truth is personal and morality is relative.

As a pastor I have spent my life teaching the church I serve to believe sound doctrine and to stand against the false teachers of our age whose views would destroy the souls of our young people. As a Christian you have every right to expect that the sermons and teaching heard in your church will reinforce the godly principles which you are trying to teach at home. But you have no right to expect your church to take the place of the home. God has given to parents the responsibility of teaching their children divine truth.

The *TAG* books have been designed to help you fulfill that assignment. The emphasis is on memorization. Some modern educators question the wisdom of teaching young children to memorize. Concern usually centers on the fear that the child is merely committing to memory meaningless words. This is a real danger—that we will be satisfied with hearing our children merely recite back to us words and sentences of which they have no understanding. That is why parents should carefully teach their children the material in these books. Personal understanding should always be the goal of our teaching. But understanding grows over time (mine has; hasn't yours?). Truth committed to memory provides the building blocks for such growth.

I originally produced the *TAG* books in the late 1990s for the parents and children in Grace Baptist Church of Cape Coral, Florida. I borrowed from and leaned on the work of many people, including Paul Settle, Fred Malone, Bill Ascol, Karen Leach, Judy Veilleux and, of course, my wife, Donna. Founders Press first published the *TAG* books in 2000 and then again in 2005. For this new edition I owe a debt of gratitude to Jared and Heather Longshore, whose determination, thoughtfulness and creativity have made this work more accessible to a new generation of parents and children. It is a testimony to God's grace in reviving the work of His gospel that they continue to find a wide readership. My prayer has been and remains that the Lord will use these books to help parents raise generations of men and women who are mighty in His Word and Spirit and who will take the wonderful news of Jesus Christ to the remaining hard places in our world.

Donna and I loved catechizing our children. Now we love watching our children who have become parents catechizing our grandchildren. It is to those children, their spouses and our grandchildren that the Truth and Grace Memory Books are dedicated.

HOW TO USE THIS MEMORY BOOK

I remember how intimidated I was when Donna and I made our first attempts to start catechizing our firstborn. After many starts and stops and lots of mistakes, we finally settled into a healthy rhythm of incorporating questions from the catechism both in set times and informal times with her and her siblings. Following are some of the lessons we learned along the way.

Discuss the material being memorized with your child. This should be done during the actual memorization as well as at other opportune times in the day. Daily experiences and observations provide a world of opportunities to illustrate and apply God's Word. For example, those pesky night frights that young children occasionally have become wonderful occasions to comfortingly remind them that, though we cannot see God, He always sees us.

Take time to define difficult terms. Question your child in order to discover the level of his understanding. When you feel that understanding is being achieved, pray with and for the child, including in your prayer some of the concepts just discussed. Expect your children to learn, and rejoice with them over their growth in knowledge and understanding of God's Word.

No matter what the age of your children, if you will begin immediately, and continue consistently, to teach them with this workbook, you will instill in them a comprehensive awareness of the Bible's whole system of revealed truth. Obviously, the earlier a child begins, the better. But these books have been designed to be useful to young people as well to children and preschoolers.

Following are some specific suggestions that come from my experience.

1. Make this workbook something very special in your child's life. Emphasize the importance of learning God's Word. If you are genuinely excited about it, most likely your children will be also.

2. Incorporate it into your regular time of family prayer and devotion. After you have read a portion of God's Word, or some Bible story book, and have prayed, take a few minutes to work on a specific verse or question. Learn to sing the hymns together as a family. You can do it! You simply have to make the effort.

3. Encourage precise memorization. If they are going to spend the time and effort to learn it, they might as well learn it accurately.

4. Be very positive. Try not to let the workbook become a battleground where a contest of the wills (child's vs. parent's) occurs. This does not mean that you let the child dictate when he will or will not work on the material. Rather, do not let yourself get into the position where you are violating biblical principles (by employing

rage, sarcasm, ridicule, empty threats, etc.) in your zeal to have your child learn the Bible! Instead, make it an enjoyable—and at times, even fun—time. Donna and I would often let our children ask us the questions.

5. Date and sign each step. At the back of the workbook there are places for the parent to signify that the student has completed the assignments. Treat each one as a significant milestone and encourage your child to keep progressing.

6. Go at your child's own rate. Children, like adults, learn differently and at different tempos. The workbook is designed so that the material can be covered as quickly or slowly as needed. Do not hesitate to move beyond the stated age levels. Remember, these are merely suggestions.

7. Discuss the content of the verses, catechism questions or hymns being learned. Help your child understand what they are saying. Remember, the goal is spiritual understanding, not mechanical regurgitation.

8. Review. Avoid placing such an emphasis on advancement that your child is tempted to utilize only his or her short-term rather than long-term memory.

9. Rejoice. Your child is learning Bible truths which some adults will never know. Thank the Lord for the privilege of teaching your children about Him. Be encouraged as you hear them reciting the Word of God and expressing important biblical truths.

10. Pray. Ask God to drive His Word deep into the heart and conscience of each child. Pray that He will send His Spirit to teach them inwardly the truth about sin and judgment, heaven and hell, Jesus and salvation. As you diligently teach your children, labor in prayer for them until you see Christ being formed in them.

11. Encourage other parents. We all need it. Make a conscious effort to give it. Training our children in the way of the Lord is a high calling. We are constantly tempted to neglect it. We all fail at some point and at some time. Resolve to be an encourager.

"

Believe me... the church of God will never be
preserved without catechesis.

"

JOHN CALVIN

HEIDELBERG CATECHISM: A BAPTIST VERSION

1. What is your only comfort in life and in death?

    That I am not my own, but belong—body and soul, in life and in death—to my faithful Savior Jesus Christ. He has fully paid for all my sins with His precious blood, and has set me free from the tyranny of the devil. He also watches over me in such a way that not a hair can fall from my head without the will of my Father in heaven; in fact, all things must work together for my salvation. Because I belong to Him, Christ, by His Holy Spirit, assures me of eternal life and makes me whole-heartedly willing and ready from now on to live for Him.

    (1 Corinthians 6:19, 20; Romans 14:7–9; 1 Corinthians 3:23; Titus 2:14; 1 Peter 1:18, 19; 1 John 1:7–9; 2:2; John 8:34–36; Hebrews 2:14, 15; 1 John 3:1–11; John 6:39, 40; 10:27–30; 2 Thessalonians 3:3; 1 Peter 1:5; Matthew

10:29–31; Luke 21:16–18; Romans 8:28; 8:15, 16; 2 Corinthians 1:21, 22; 5:5; Ephesians 1:13, 14; Romans 8:1–17)

2. What must you know to live and die in the joy of this comfort?

Three things: first, how great my sin and misery are; second, how I am set free from all my sins and misery; third, how I am to thank God for such deliverance.

(Romans 3:9; 10; 1 John 1:10; John 17:3; Acts 4:12; 10:43; Matthew 5:16; Romans 6:13; Ephesians 5:8–10; 2 Timothy 2:15; 1 Peter 2:9, 10)

3. How do you come to know your misery?

The law of God tells me.

(Romans 3:20; 7:7–25)

4. What does God's law require of us?

Christ teaches us this in summary in Matthew 22—You shall love the Lord your God with all your heart, with all your soul, and with all your mind. This is the great and first commandment. And a second is like it, you shall love your neighbor as yourself. On these two commandments hang all the law and the prophets.

(Deuteronomy 6:5; Leviticus 19:18)

5. Can you live up to all this perfectly?

    No. I have a natural tendency to hate God and my neighbor.

    (Romans 3:9–20, 23; 1 John 1:8, 10; Genesis 6:5; Jeremiah 17:9; Romans 7:23, 24; 8:7; Ephesians 2:1–3; Titus 3:3)

6. Did God create man wicked and perverse?

    No. God created man good, and in His own image, that is, in true righteousness and holiness, so that he might truly know God his creator, love Him with all his heart, and live with Him in eternal happiness for His praise and glory.

    (Genesis 1:31; 1:26, 27; Ephesians 4:24; Colossians 3:10; Psalm 8)

7. Then where does man's corrupt nature come from?

    From the fall and disobedience of our first parents, Adam and Eve, in Paradise. This fall has so poisoned our nature that we are all born sinners—corrupt from conception on.

    (Genesis 3; Romans 5:12, 18, 19; Psalm 51:5)

8. But are we so corrupt that we are totally unable to do any good and inclined toward all evil?

Yes, unless we are born again, by the Spirit of God.

(Genesis 6:5; 8:21; Job 14:4; Isaiah 53:6; John 3:3–5)

9. But doesn't God do man an injustice by requiring in His law what man is unable to do?

No, God created man with the ability to keep the law. Man, however, when tempted by the devil, in reckless disobedience, robbed himself and his descendants of these gifts.

(Genesis 1:31; Ephesians 4:24; Genesis 3:13; John 8:44; Genesis 3:6; Romans 5:12, 18, 19)

10. Will God permit such disobedience and rebellion to go unpunished?

Certainly not. He is terribly angry about the sin we are born with as well as the sins we personally commit. As a just judge He punishes them now and in eternity. He has declared: "Cursed is the one who does not confirm all the words of this law."

(Exodus 34:7; Psalm 5:4–6; Nahum 1:2; Romans 1:18; Ephesians 5:6; Hebrews 9:27; Deuteronomy 27:26; Galatians 3:10)

11.   But isn't God also merciful?

       God is certainly merciful, but He is also just. His justice demands that sin, committed against His supreme majesty, be punished with the supreme penalty—eternal punishment of body and soul.

       (Exodus 34:6, 7; Psalm 103:8, 9; Exodus 34:7; Deuteronomy 7:9–11; Psalm 5:4–6; Hebrews 10:30, 31; Matthew 25:35–46)

12.   According to God's righteous judgment we deserve punishment both in this world and forever after: how can we escape this punishment and return to God's favor?

       God requires that His justice be satisfied. Therefore the claims of His justice must be paid in full, either by ourselves or by another.

       (Exodus 23:7; Romans 2:1–11; Isaiah 53:11; Romans 8:3, 4)

13.   Can we pay this debt ourselves?

       Certainly not. Actually, we increase our guilt every day.

       (Matthew 6:12; Romans 2:4, 5)

14. Can another creature—any at all— pay this debt for us?

No. To begin with, God will not punish another creature for man's guilt. Besides, no mere creature can bear the weight of God's eternal anger against sin and release others from it.

(Ezekiel 18:4, 20; Hebrews 2:14–18; Psalm 49:7–9; 130:3)

15. What kind of Mediator and Deliverer should we look for then?

He must be truly human and truly righteous, yet more powerful than all creatures, that is, He must also be truly God.

(Romans 1:3; 2 Corinthians 15:21; Hebrews 2:17; Isaiah 53:9; 2 Corinthians 5:21; Hebrews 7:26; Isaiah 7:14; 9:6; Jeremiah 23:6; John 1:1)

16. Why must He be truly human and truly righteous?

God's justice demands it: man has sinned, man must pay for his sin, but a sinner cannot pay for others.

(Romans 5:12, 15; 1 Corinthians 15:21; Hebrews 2:14–16; 7:26, 27; 1 Peter 3:18)

17. Why must He also be truly God?

So that, by the power of His divinity, He might bear the weight of God's anger in His humanity and earn for us and restore to us righteousness and life.

(Isaiah 53; John 3:16; 2 Corinthians 5:21)

18. And who is this Mediator, who is truly God and at the same time truly human and truly righteous?

Our Lord Jesus Christ, who was given us to set us completely free and to make us right with God.

(Matthew 1:21–23; Luke 2:11; 1 Timothy 2:5; 1 Corinthians 1:30)

19. How do you come to know this?

The holy gospel tells me. God Himself began to reveal the gospel already in Paradise; later, He proclaimed it by the holy patriarchs and prophets, and portrayed it by the sacrifices and other ceremonies of the law; finally, He fulfilled it through His own dear Son.

(Genesis 3:15; 22:18; 49:10; Isaiah 53; Jeremiah 23:5, 6; Micah 7:18–20; Acts 10:43; Hebrews 1:1, 2; Leviticus 1–7; John 5:46; Hebrews 10:1–10; Romans 10:4 Galatians 4:4, 5; Colossians 2:17)

20. Are all men saved through Christ just as all were lost through Adam?

No. Only those are saved who by true faith are grafted into Christ and by grace receive all His blessings.

(Matthew 7:14; John 3:16, 18, 36: Romans 11:16–21)

21. What is true faith?

True faith is not only a knowledge and conviction that everything God reveals in His Word is true; it is also a deep-rooted assurance, created in me by the Holy Spirit through the gospel that, out of sheer grace earned for us by Christ, not only others, but I too, have had my sins forgiven, have been made forever right with God, and have been granted salvation.

(John 17:3, 17; Hebrews 11:1–3; James 2:19; Romans 4:18–21; 5:1; 10:10; Hebrews 4:14–16; Matthew 16:15–17; John 3:5; Acts 16:14; Romans 1:16; 10:17; 1 Corinthians 1:21; Romans 3:21–26; Galatians 2:16; Ephesians 2:8–10; Galatians 2:20; Romans 1:17; Hebrews 10:10)

22. What then must a Christian believe?

Everything God promises us in the gospel. That gospel is summarized for us in the articles of our Christian faith—a creed beyond doubt, and confessed throughout the world.

(Matthew 28:18–20; John 20:30, 31)

23. What are these articles?

I believe in God the Father, almighty, maker of heaven and earth. And in Jesus Christ, His only begotten Son, our Lord; who was conceived by the Holy Spirit, born of the virgin Mary; suffered under Pontius Pilate; was crucified, dead and buried; He descended into hell; the third day He rose again from the dead; He ascended into heaven, and sitteth at the right hand of God the Father almighty; from there He shall come to judge the living and the dead. I believe in the Holy Spirit; I believe a holy universal church, the communion of saints; the forgiveness of sins; the resurrection of the body; and the life everlasting.

24. How are these articles divided?

Into three parts: God the Father and our creation; God the Son and our deliverance; God the Holy Spirit and our sanctification.

25. Since there is but one God, why do you speak of three: Father, Son, and Holy Spirit?

Because that is how God has revealed Himself in His Word: these three distinct persons are one, true, eternal God.

(Deuteronomy 6:4; 1 Corinthians 8:4, 6; Matthew 3:16, 17; 28:18, 19; Luke 4:18 [Isaiah 61:1]; John 14:26; 15:26; 2 Corinthians 13:14; Galatians 4:6; Titus 3:5, 6)

26. What do you believe when you say: "I believe in God the Father, almighty, maker of heaven and earth?

That the eternal Father of our Lord Jesus Christ, who out of nothing created heaven and earth and everything in them, who still upholds and rules them by His eternal counsel and providence, is my God and Father because of Christ His Son. I trust Him so much that I do not doubt He will provide whatever I need for body and soul, and He will turn to my good whatever adversity He sends me in this sad world. He is able to do this because He is almighty God; He desires to do this because He is a faithful Father.

(Genesis 1 & 2; Exodus 20:11; Psalm 33:6; Isaiah 44:24; 14:15; Psalm 104; Matthew 6:30; 10:29; Ephesians 1:11; John 1:12, 13; Romans 8:15, 16; Galatians 4:4–7; Ephesians 1:5; Psalm 55:22; Matthew 6:25, 26; Luke 12:22–31; Romans 8:28; Genesis 18:14; Romans 8:31–39; Matthew 7:9–11)

27. What do you understand by the providence of God?

Providence is the almighty and ever present power of God by which He upholds, as with His hand, heaven and earth and all creatures, and so rules them that leaf and blade, rain and drought, fruitful and lean years, food and drink, health and sickness, prosperity and poverty—all things, in fact, come to us not by chance but from His fatherly hand.

(Jeremiah 23:23, 24; Acts 17:24–28; Hebrews 1:3; Jeremiah 5:24; Acts 14:15–17; John 9:3; Proverbs 22:2; 16:33; Matthew 10:29)

28. How does the knowledge of God's creation and providence help us?

We can be patient when things go against us, thankful when things go well, and for the future we can have good confidence in our faithful God and Father that nothing will separate us from His love. All creatures are so completely in His hand that without His will they can neither move nor be moved.

(Job 1:21, 22; James 1:3; Deuteronomy 8:10; 1 Thessalonians 5:18; Psalm 55:22; Romans 5:3–5; 8:38, 39; Job 1:12; 2:6; Proverbs 21:1; Acts 17:24–28)

29. Why is the Son of God called "Jesus" meaning "Savior"?

    Because He saves us from our sins. Salvation cannot be found in anyone else; it is futile to look for any salvation elsewhere.

    (Matthew 1:21; Hebrews 7:25; Isaiah 43:11; John 15:5; Acts 4:11, 12; 1 Timothy 2:5)

30. Do those who look for their salvation and security in saints, in themselves, or elsewhere really believe in the only Savior Jesus?

    No. Although they boast of being His, by their deeds they deny the only Savior and Deliverer, Jesus. Either Jesus is not a perfect Savior, or those who in true faith accept this Savior have in Him all they need for their salvation.

    (1 Corinthians 1:12, 13; Galatians 5:4; Colossians 1:19, 20; 2:10; 1 John 1:7)

31.   Why is He called "Christ" meaning "Anointed"?

Because He has been ordained by God the Father and has been anointed with the Holy Spirit to be our chief Prophet and Teacher who perfectly reveals to us the secret counsel and will of God for our deliverance; our only High Priest who has set us free by the one sacrifice of His body, and who continually pleads our cause with the Father; and our eternal King who governs us by His Word and Spirit, and who guards us and keeps us in the freedom He has won for us.

(Luke 3:21, 22; 4:14–19 [Isaiah 61:1]; Hebrews 1:9 [Psalm 45:7]; Acts 3:22 [Deuteronomy 18:15]; John 1:18; 15:15; Hebrews 7:17 [Psalm 110:4]; Hebrews 9:12; 10:11–14; Romans 8:34; Hebrews 9:24; Matthew 21:5 [Zechariah 9:9]; Matthew 28:18–20; John 10:28; Revelation 12:10, 11)

32.   But why are you called a Christian?

Because by faith I am a member of Christ and so I share in His anointing. I am anointed to confess His name, to present myself to Him as a living sacrifice of thanks, to strive with a good conscience against sin and the devil in this life, and afterward to reign with Christ over all creation for all eternity.

(1 Corinthians 12:12–29; Acts 2:17 [Joel 2:28]; 1 John 2:27; Matthew 10:32; Romans 10:9, 10; Hebrews 13:15; Romans 12:1; 1 Peter 2:5, 9; Galatians 5:16, 17; Ephesians 6:11; 1 Timothy 1:18, 19; Matthew 25:34; 2 Timothy 2:12)

33. Why is He called God's "only begotten Son" when we also are God's children?

Because Christ alone is the eternal, natural Son of God. We, however, are adopted children of God—adopted by grace through Christ.

(John 1:1–3, 14, 18; Hebrews 1; John 1:12; Romans 8:14–17; Ephesians 1:5, 6)

34. Why do you call Him Lord?

Because—not with gold or silver, but with His precious blood—He has set us free from sin and from the tyranny of the devil, and has bought us, body and soul, to be His very own.

(1 Peter 1:18, 19; Colossians 1:13, 14; Hebrews 2:14, 15; 1 Corinthians 6:20; 1 Timothy 2:5, 6)

35. What does it mean that He "was conceived by the Holy Spirit, born of the virgin Mary"?

That the eternal Son of God, who is and remains true and eternal God, took to Himself, through the working of the Holy Spirit, from the flesh and blood of the virgin Mary, a truly human nature so that He might become David's true descendant, in all things like us except for sin.

(John 1:1; 10:30–36; Acts 13:33 [Psalm 2:7]; Colossians 1:15–17; 1 John 5:20; Luke 1:35; Matthew 1:18–23; John 1:14; Galatians 4:4; Hebrews 2:14; 2 Samuel 7:12–16; Psalm 132:11; Matthew 1:1; Romans 1:3; Philippians 2:7; Hebrews 2:17; Hebrews 4:15; 7:26,27)

36. How does the holy conception and birth of Christ benefit you?

He is our Mediator, and with His innocence and perfect holiness He removes from God's sight my sin—mine since I was conceived.

(1 Timothy 2:5, 6; Hebrews 9:13–15; Romans 8:3, 4; 2 Corinthians 5:21; Galatians 4:4, 5; 1 Peter 1:18, 19)

37. What do you understand by the word "suffered"?

That during His whole life on earth, but especially at the end, Christ sustained in body and soul the anger of God against the sin of the whole human race. This He did in order that, by His suffering as the only atoning sacrifice, He might set us free, body and soul, from eternal condemnation, and gain for us God's grace, righteousness, and eternal life.

(Isaiah 53; 1 Peter 2:24; 3:18; Romans 3:25; Hebrews 10:14; 1 John 2:2; 4:10; Romans 8:1–4; Galatians 3:13; John 3:16; Romans 3:24–26)

38. Why did He suffer "under Pontius Pilate" as judge?

So that He, though innocent, might be condemned by a civil judge, and so free us from the severe judgment of God that was to fall on us.

(Luke 23:13–24; John 19:4, 12–16; Isaiah 53:4, 5; 2 Corinthians 5:21; Galatians 3:13)

39. Is it significant that He was "crucified" instead of dying some other way?

Yes. This death convinces me that He shouldered the curse which lay on me, since death by crucifixion was accursed by God.

(Galatians 3:10–13 [Deuteronomy 21:23])

40. Why did Christ have to go all the way to death?

Because God's justice and truth demand it: only the death of God's Son could pay for our sins.

(Genesis 2:17; Romans 8:3, 4; Philippians 2:8; Hebrews 2:9)

41. Why was He "buried"?

His burial testifies that He really died.

(Isaiah 53:9; John 19:38–42; Acts 13:29; 1 Corinthians 15:3, 4)

42. Since Christ has died for us, why do we still have to die?

Our death does not pay the debt of our sins. Rather, it puts an end to our sinning and is our entrance into eternal life.

(Psalm 49:7; John 5:24; Philippians 1:21–23; 1 Thessalonians 5:9, 10)

43. What further advantage do we receive from Christ's sacrifice and death on the cross?

Through Christ's death our old selves are crucified, put to death, and buried with Him, so that the evil desires of the flesh may no longer rule us, but that instead we may dedicate ourselves as an offering of gratitude to Him.

(Romans 6:5–11; Colossians 2:11, 12; Romans 6:12–14; Romans 12:1; Ephesians 5:1, 2)

44. How does Christ's resurrection benefit us?

First, by His resurrection He has overcome death, so that He might make us share in the righteousness He won for us by His death; second, by His power we too are already now resurrected to a new life; third, Christ's resurrection is a guarantee of our glorious resurrection.

(Romans 4:25; 1 Corinthians 15:16–20; 1 Peter 1:3–5; Romans 6:5–11; Ephesians 2:4–6; Colossians 3:1–4; Romans 8:11; 1 Corinthians 15:12–23; Phil. 3:20, 21)

45. What do you mean by saying: "He ascended into heaven"?

That Christ, while His disciples watched, was lifted up from the earth into heaven and will be there for our good until He comes again to judge the living and the dead.

(Luke 24:50, 51; Acts 1:9–11; Romans 8:34; Ephesians 4:8–18; Hebrews 7:23–25; 9:24; Acts 1:11)

46. But isn't Christ with us until the end of the world as He promised us?

    Christ is true man and true God. In His human nature Christ is not now on earth; but in His divinity, majesty, grace, and Spirit He is not absent from us for a moment.

    (Matthew 28:20; Acts 1:9–11; 3:19–21; Matthew 28:18–20; John 14:16–19)

47. If His humanity is not present wherever His divinity is, then aren't the two natures of Christ separated from each other?

    Certainly not. Since divinity is not limited and is present everywhere, it is evident that Christ's divinity is surely beyond the bounds of the humanity He has taken on, but at the same time His divinity is in and remains personally united to His humanity.

    (Jeremiah 23:23, 24; Acts 7:48, 49 [Isaiah 66:1]; John 1:14; 3:13; Colossians 2:9)

48. How does Christ's ascension into heaven benefit us?

First, He pleads our cause in heaven in the presence of His Father; second, we have our own flesh in heaven—a guarantee that Christ our head will take us, His members, to Himself in heaven; third, He sends His Spirit to us on earth as further guarantee. By the Spirit's power we make the goal of our lives, not earthly things, but the things above where Christ is, sitting at God's right hand.

(Romans 8:34; 1 John 2:1; John 14:2; 17:24; Ephesians 2:4–6; John 14:16; 2 Corinthians 1:21, 22; 5:5; Colossians 3:1–4)

49. Why the next words: "and sits at the right hand of God"?

Christ ascended to heaven, there to show that He is head of His church, and that the Father rules all things through Him.

(Ephesians 1:20–23; Colossians 1:18; Matthew 28:18; John 5:22, 23)

50. How does this glory of Christ our head benefit us?

First, through His Holy Spirit He pours out His gifts from heaven upon us His members; second, by His power He defends us and keeps us safe from all enemies.

(Acts 2:33; Ephesians 4:7–12; Psalm 110:1, 2; John 10:27–30; Revelation 19:11–16)

51. How does Christ's return "to judge the living and the dead" comfort you?

In all my distress and persecution I turn my eyes to the heavens and confidently await as judge the very One who has already stood trial in my place before God and so removed the whole curse from me. All His enemies and mine He will condemn to everlasting punishment: but me and all His chosen ones He will take along with Him into the joy and the glory of heaven.

(Luke 21:28; Romans 8:22–25; Philippians 3:20, 21; Titus 2:13, 14; Matthew 25:31–46; 2 Thessalonians 1:6–10)

52. What do you believe concerning "the Holy Spirit"?

First, He, as well as the Father and the Son, is eternal God; second, He has been given to me personally, so that, by true faith, He makes me share in Christ and all His blessings, comforts me, and remains with me forever.

(Genesis 1:1, 2; Matthew 28:19; Acts 5:3, 4; 1 Corinthians 6:19; 2 Corinthians 1:21, 22; Galatians 4:6; 3:14; John 15:26; Acts 9:31; John 14:16, 17; 1 Peter 4:14)

53. What do you believe concerning the "Holy Catholic Church"?

I believe that the Son of God through His Spirit and Word, out of the entire human race, from the beginning of the world to its end, gathers, protects, and preserves for Himself a community chosen for eternal life and united in true faith. And of this community I am and always will be a living member.

(John 10:14–16; Acts 20:28; Romans 10:14–17; Colossians 1:18; Genesis 26:3b, 4; Revelation 5:9; Isaiah 59:21; 1 Corinthians 11:26; Matthew 16:18; John 10:28–30; Romans 8:28–30; Ephesians 1:3–14; Acts 2:42–47; Ephesians 4:1–6; 1 John 3:14, 19–21; John 10:27, 28; 1 Corinthians 1:4–9; 1 Peter 1:3–5)

54. What do you understand by "the communion of saints"?

First, that believers one and all, as members of this community, share in Christ and in all His treasures and gifts; second, that each member should consider it his duty to use his gifts readily and cheerfully for the service and enrichment of the other members.

(Romans 8:32; 1 Corinthians 6:17; 12:4–7, 12, 13; 1 John 1:3; Romans 12:4–8; 1 Corinthians 12:20–27; 13:1–7; Philippians 2:4–8)

55. What do you believe concerning "the forgiveness of sins"?

I believe that God because of Christ's atonement, will never hold against me any of my sins nor my sinful nature which I need to struggle against all my life. Rather, in His grace God grants me the righteousness of Christ to free me forever from judgment.

(Psalm 103:3, 4, 10, 12; Micah 7:18, 19; 2 Corinthians 5:18–21; 1 John 1:7; 2:2; Romans 7:21–25; John 3:17, 18; Romans 8:1, 2)

56. How does "the resurrection of the body" comfort you?

Not only my soul will be taken immediately after this life to Christ its head, but even my very flesh, raised by the power of Christ, will be reunited with my soul and made like Christ's glorious body.

(Luke 23:43; Philippians 1:21–23; 1 Corinthians 15:20, 42–46, 54; Philippians 3:21; 1 John 3:2)

57. How does the article concerning "life everlasting" comfort you?

Even as I already now experience in my heart the beginning of eternal joy, so after this life I will have perfect blessedness such as no eye has seen, no ear heard, no man has ever imagined: a blessedness in which to praise God eternally.

(Romans 14:17; John 17:3; 1 Corinthians 2:9)

58. What good does it do you, however, to believe all this?

In Christ I am right with God and heir to life everlasting.

(John 3:36; Romans 1:17 [Habakkuk 2:4]; Romans 5:1, 2)

59. How are you right with God?

Only by true faith in Jesus Christ. Even though my conscience accuses me of having grievously sinned against all God's commandments and of never having kept any of them, and even though I am still inclined toward all evil, nevertheless, without my deserving it at all, out of sheer grace, God grants and credits to me the perfect satisfaction, righteousness, and holiness of Christ, as if I had never sinned nor been a sinner, as if I had been as perfectly obedient as Christ was obedient for me. All I need to do is to receive this gift of God with a repentant and believing heart.

(Romans 3:21–28; Galatians 2:16; Ephesians 2:8, 9; Philippians 3:8–11; Romans 3:9, 10; 7:23; Titus 3:4, 5; Romans 3:24; Ephesians 2:8; Romans 4:3–5 [Genesis 15:6]; 2 Corinthians 5:17–19; 1 John 2:1, 2; Romans 4:24, 25; 2 Corinthians 5:21; John 3:18; Acts 16:30, 31)

60. Why do you say that by faith alone you are right with God?

It is not because of any value my faith has that God is pleased with me. Only Christ's satisfaction, righteousness, and holiness make me right with God. And I can receive this righteousness and make it mine in no other way than by faith alone.

(1 Corinthians 1:30, 31; Romans 10:10; 1 John 5:10–12)

61. Why can't the good we do make us right with God, or at least help make us right with Him?

Because the righteousness which can pass God's scrutiny must be entirely perfect and must in every way measure up to the divine law. Even the very best we do in this life is imperfect and stained with sin.

(Romans 3:20; Galatians 3:10 [Deuteronomy 27:26]; Isaiah 64:6)

62. How can you say that the good we do doesn't earn anything when God promises to reward it in this life and the next?

This reward is not earned; it is a gift of grace.

(Matthew 5:12; Hebrews 11:6; Luke 17:10; 2 Timothy 4:7, 8)

63. But doesn't this teaching make people indifferent and wicked?

No. It is impossible for those grafted into Christ by true faith not to produce fruits of gratitude.

(Luke 6:43–45; John 15:5)

64. You confess that by faith alone you share in Christ and all His blessings: where does faith come from?

The Holy Spirit produces it in our hearts by the preaching of the holy gospel, confirms it through our use of the holy sacraments, and strengthens it through prayer and Scripture reading.

(John 3:5; 1 Corinthians 2:10–14; Ephesians 2:8; Romans 10:17; 1 Peter 1:23–25; Matthew 28:19, 20; 1 Corinthians 10:16; Ephesians 3:14–21; 1 Peter 2:1–2)

65. What are sacraments (or ordinances)?

Sacraments (or ordinances) are holy signs for believers. They were instituted by God so that by our use of them He might make us understand more clearly the promise of the gospel. And this is God's gospel promise: to forgive our sins and give us eternal life by grace alone because of Christ's one sacrifice finished on the cross.

(Genesis 17:11; Deuteronomy 30:6; Romans 4:11; Matthew 26:27, 28; Hebrews 10:10; Acts 2:38)

66. Are both the Word and the sacraments then intended to focus our faith on the sacrifice of Jesus Christ on the cross as the only ground of our salvation?

Right! In the gospel the Holy Spirit teaches us and through the holy sacraments He assures us that our entire salvation rests on Christ's one sacrifice for us on the cross.

(Romans 6:3; 1 Corinthians 11:26; Galatians 3:27)

67. How many sacraments did Christ institute in the New Testament?

Two: baptism and the Lord's supper.

(Matthew 28:19, 20; 1 Corinthians 23:26)

68. What is Baptism?

Baptism is the immersion of a believer into water as a sign of his union with Jesus Christ and salvation by God's grace.

(Matthew 28:19; Acts 8:36–39)

69. What does baptism symbolize?

My death, burial and resurrection with the Lord Jesus Christ.

(Romans 6:1–4)

70. Who should be baptized?

Those who, having been born of God's Spirit, repent of their sins and believe in Jesus Christ for salvation. In other words, only believers should be baptized.

(Acts 2:41–42; Matthew 28:19)

71. What is the Lord's Supper?

The Lord's Supper is the declaration of Christ's death by believers through the giving and receiving of bread and the fruit of the vine.

(1 Corinthians 11:23–26; Luke 22)

72. How does the Lord's supper remind you and assure you that you share in Christ's one sacrifice on the cross and in all His gifts?

In this way: Christ has commanded me and all believers to eat this broken bread and to drink this cup. With this command He gave this promise: First, as surely as I see with my eyes the bread of the Lord broken for me and the cup given to me, so surely His body was offered and broken for me on the cross. Second, as surely as I receive from the hand of him who serves, and taste with my mouth the bread and cup of the Lord, given me as sure signs of Christ's body and blood, so surely He nourishes and refreshes my soul for eternal life with His crucified body and poured-out blood.

(Matthew 26:26–28; Mark 14:22–24; Luke 22:19, 20; 1 Corinthians 11:23–25)

73. Are the bread and fruit of the vine changed into the real body and blood of Christ?

No. Just as the water of baptism is not changed into Christ's blood and does not itself wash away sins but is a sign of our union with Christ, so too the bread and fruit of the vine of the Lord's supper are not changed into the actual body and blood of Christ in keeping with the nature and language of sacraments.

(Ephesians 5:26; Titus 3:5; Matthew 26:26–29; 1 Corinthians 10:16, 17; 11:26–28; Genesis 17:10, 11; Exodus 12:11; 1 Corinthians 10:1–4)

74. Why then does Christ call the bread His body and the cup His blood, or the new covenant in His blood?

Christ has good reason for these words. He wants to teach us that He established the new covenant by His death and that as bread and drink nourish our temporal life, so too His crucified body and poured-out blood truly nourish our souls for eternal life. But more important, He wants to assure us, by this visible sign and pledge, that we, through the Holy Spirit's work, share in His true body and blood as surely as our mouths receive these holy signs in His remembrance, and that all of His suffering and obedience are as definitely ours as if we personally had suffered and paid for our sins.

(John 6:51, 55; 1 Corinthians 10:16,17; 11:26; Romans 6:5–11)

75. Who are to come to the Lord's table?

Those baptized believers who are displeased with themselves because of their sins, but who nevertheless trust that their sins are pardoned and that their continuing weakness is covered by the suffering and death of Christ, and who also desire more and more to strengthen their faith and to lead a better life. Hypocrites and those who are unrepentant, however, eat and drink judgment on themselves.

(1 Corinthians 10:19–22; 11:26–32)

76. Are those who show by what they say and do that they are unbelieving and ungodly to be admitted to the Lord's supper?
No, that would dishonor God's covenant and bring down God's anger upon the entire congregation. Therefore, according to the instruction of Christ and His apostles, the Christian church is duty-bound to exclude such people, by the official use of the keys of the kingdom, until they repent of their sins.

(1 Corinthians 11:17–32; Psalm 50:14–16; Isaiah 1:11–17)

77. What are the keys of the kingdom?
The preaching of the holy gospel and Christian discipline toward repentance. Both preaching and discipline open the kingdom of heaven to believers and close it to unbelievers.

(Matthew 16:19; John 20:22, 23)

78. How does preaching the gospel open and close the kingdom of heaven?

According to the command of Christ: The kingdom of heaven is opened by proclaiming and publicly declaring to each and every believer that, as often as he accepts the gospel promise in true faith, God, because of what Christ has done, truly forgives all his sins. The kingdom of heaven is closed, however, by proclaiming and publicly declaring to unbelievers and hypocrites that, as long as they do not repent, the anger of God and eternal condemnation rest on them. God's judgment, both in this life and in the life to come, is based on this gospel testimony.

(Matthew 16:19; John 3:31–36; 20:21–23)

79. How is the kingdom of heaven closed and opened by Christian discipline?

According to the command of Christ: If anyone, though called a Christian, professes unchristian teachings or lives an unchristian life, if after repeated brotherly counsel, he refuses to abandon his errors and wickedness, and, if after being reported to the church he fails to respond also to their admonition—such a one the church must exclude from the Christian fellowship and God Himself excludes him from the kingdom of Christ. Such a person, when he promises and demonstrates genuine repentance, is

received again as a member of Christ and of
His church.

(Matthew 18:15–20; 1 Corinthians 5:3–5, 11–
13; 2 Thessalonians 3:14, 15; Luke 15:20–24;
2 Corinthians 2:6–11)

80. We have been delivered from our misery by
God's grace alone through Christ and not
because we have earned it: Why then must
we still do good?

To be sure, Christ has redeemed us by His
blood. But we do good because Christ by His
Spirit is also renewing us to be like Himself,
so that in all our living we may show that we
are thankful to God for all He has done for
us, and so that He may be praised through
us. And we do good so that we may be
assured of our faith by its fruits, and so that
by our godly living our neighbors may be
won over to Christ.

(Romans 6:13; 12:1, 2; 1 Peter 2:5–10;
Matthew 5:16; 1 Corinthians 6:19, 20;
Matthew 7:17, 18; Galatians 5:22–24; 2 Peter
1:10, 11; Matthew 5:14–16; Romans 14:17–19;
1 Peter 2:12; 3:1, 2)

81. Can those be saved who do not turn to God from their ungrateful and impenitent ways?

By no means. Scripture tells us that no unchaste person, no idolater, adulterer, thief, no covetous person, no drunkard, slanderer, robber, or the like is going to inherit the kingdom of God.

(1 Corinthians 6:9, 10; Galatians 5:19–21; Ephesians 5:1–20; 1 John 3:14)

82. What is involved in genuine repentance or conversion?

Two things: the dying-away of the old self, and the coming-to-life of the new.

(Romans 6:1–11; 2 Corinthians 5:17; Ephesians 4:22–24; Colossians 3:5–10)

83. What is the dying-away of the old self?

It is to be genuinely sorry for sin, to hate it more and more, and to run away from it.

(Psalm 51:3, 4, 17; Joel 2:12, 13; Romans 8:12, 13; 2 Corinthians 7:10)

84. What is the coming-to-life of the new self?

It is a wholehearted joy in God through Christ and a delight to do every kind of good as God wants us to.

(Psalm 51:8, 12; Isaiah 57:15; Romans 5:1; 14:17; 6:10, 11; Galatians 2:20)

85. What do we do that is good?

Only that which arises out of true faith, conforms to God's law, and is done for His glory; and not that which is based on what we think is right or on established human tradition.

(John 15:5; Hebrews 11:6; Leviticus 18:4 1 Samuel 15:22; Ephesians 2:10; 1 Corinthians 10:31; Deuteronomy 12:32; Isaiah 29:13; Ezekiel 20:18, 19; Matthew 15:7–9)

86. What does the Lord say in His law?

God spoke all these words:

I am the Lord your God, who brought you out of the land of Egypt, out of the house of bondage. You shall have no other gods before Me.

You shall not make for yourself a graven image, or any likeness of anything that is in heaven above, or that is in the earth beneath, or that is in the water under the earth; you shall not bow down to them or serve them; for I the Lord your God am a jealous God, visiting the iniquity of the fathers upon the children to the third and the fourth generation of those who hate Me, but showing steadfast love to thousands of those who love Me and keep My commandments.

You shall not take the name of the Lord your God in vain; for the Lord will not hold him guiltless who takes His name in vain.

Remember the Sabbath day, to keep it holy. Six days you shall labor, and do all your work; but the seventh day is a Sabbath to the Lord your God; in it you shall not do any work, you, or your son, or your daughter, your manservant, or your maidservant, or your cattle, or the sojourner who is within your gates; for in six days the Lord made heaven and earth, the sea, and all that is in them, and rested the seventh day; therefore the Lord blessed the Sabbath day and hallowed it.

Honor your father and your mother, that your days may be long in the land which the Lord your God gives you.

You shall not kill.

You shall not commit adultery.

You shall not steal.

You shall not bear false witness against your neighbor.

You shall not covet your neighbor's house; you shall not covet your neighbor's wife, or his manservant, or his maidservant, or his ox, or his ass, or anything that is your neighbor's.
(Exodus 20:1–17; Deuteronomy 5:6–21)

87. How are these commandments divided?

Into two tables. The first has four commandments, teaching us what our relation to God should be. The second has six commandments, teaching us what we owe our neighbor.

(Matthew 22:37–39)

88. What does the Lord require in the first commandment?

That I, not wanting to endanger my very salvation, avoid and shun all idolatry, magic, superstitious rites, and prayer to saints or the other creatures. That I sincerely acknowledge the only true God, trust Him alone, look to Him for every good thing humbly and patiently, love Him, fear Him, and honor Him with all my heart. In short, that I give up anything rather than go against His will in any way.

(1 Corinthians 6:9,10; 10:5–14; 1 John 5:21; Leviticus 19:31; Deuteronomy 18:9–12; Matthew 4:10; Revelation 19:10; 22:8, 9; John 17:3; Jeremiah 17: 5, 7; Psalm 104:27, 28; James 1:17; 1 Peter 5:5, 6; Colossians 1:11; Hebrews 10:36; Matthew 2:37 [Deuteronomy 6:50]; Proverbs 9:10; 1 Peter 1:17; Matthew 4:10 [Deuteronomy 6:13]; Matthew 5:29, 30; 10:37–39)

89. What is idolatry?

Idolatry is having or inventing something in which one trusts in place of or alongside of the only true God, who has revealed Himself in His Word.

(1 Chronicles 16:26; Galatians 4:8, 9; Ephesians 5:5; Phil. 3:19)

90. What is God's will for us in the second commandment?
That we in no way make any image of God nor worship Him in any other way than He has commanded in His Word.

(Deuteronomy 4:15–19; Isaiah 40:18–25; Acts 17:29; Romans 1:23; Leviticus 10:1–7; 1 Samuel 15:22, 23; John 4:23, 24)

91. May we then not make any image at all?

God can not and may not be visibly portrayed in any way. Although creatures may be portrayed, yet God forbids making or having such images if one's intention is to worship them or to serve God through them.

(Exodus 34:13, 14, 17; 2 Kings 18:4, 5)

92. But may not images be permitted in the churches as teaching aids for the unlearned?

No, we shouldn't try to be wiser than God. He wants His people instructed by the living preaching of His Word—not by idols that cannot even talk.

(Romans 10:14, 15, 17; 2 Timothy 3:16, 17; 2 Peter 1:19; Jeremiah 10:8; Habakkuk 2:18–20)

93. What is God's will for us in the third commandment?

That we neither blaspheme nor misuse the name of God by cursing, perjury, or unnecessary oaths, nor share in such horrible sins by being silent bystanders. In a word, it requires that we use the holy name of God only with reverence and awe, so that we may properly confess Him, pray to Him, and praise Him in everything we do and say.

(Leviticus 24:10–17; Leviticus 19:12; Matthew 5:37; James 5:12; Leviticus 5:1; Proverbs 29:24; Psalm 99:1–5; Jeremiah 4:2; Matthew 10:32, 33: Romans 10:9, 10; Psalm 50:14, 15; 1 Timothy 2:8; Colossians 3:17)

94. Is blasphemy of God's name by swearing and cursing really such serious sin that God is angry also with those who do not do all they can to help prevent it and to forbid it?

Yes, indeed. No sin is greater, no sin makes God more angry than blaspheming His name. That is why He commanded the death penalty for it.

(Leviticus 5:1; 24:10–17)

95. But may we swear an oath in God's name if we do it reverently?

Yes, when the government demands it, or when necessity requires it, in order to maintain and promote truth and trustworthiness for God's glory and our neighbor's good. Such oaths are approved in God's Word and were rightly used by Old and New Testament believers.

(Deuteronomy 6:13; 10:20; Jeremiah 4:1, 2; Hebrews 6:16; Genesis 21:24; Joshua 9:15; 1 Kings 1:29, 30; Romans 1:9; 2 Corinthians 1:23)

96. May we swear by saints or other creatures?

No. A legitimate oath means calling upon God as the One who knows my heart to witness to my truthfulness and to punish me if I swear falsely. No creature is worthy of such honor.

(Romans 9:1; 2 Corinthians 1:23; Matthew 5:34–37; 23:16–22; James 5:12)

97. What is God's will for us in the fourth commandment?

First, that the gospel ministry and education for it be maintained, and that, especially on the festive day of rest, I regularly attend the assembly of God's people to learn what God's Word teaches, to participate in the sacraments, to pray to God publicly, and to bring Christian offerings for the poor. Second, that every day of my life I rest from my evil ways, let the Lord work in me through His Spirit, and so begin already in this life the eternal Sabbath.

(Deuteronomy 6:4–9, 20–25; 1 Corinthians 9:13, 14; 2 Timothy 2:2; 3:13–17; Titus 1:5; Deuteronomy 12:5–12; Psalm 40:9, 10; 68:26; Acts 2:42–47; Hebrews 10:23–25; Romans 10:14–17; 1 Corinthians 14:31, 32; 1 Timothy 4:13; 1 Corinthians 11:23, 24; Colossians 3:16; 1 Timothy 2:1; Psalm 50:14; 1 Corinthians 16:2; 2 Corinthians 8, 9; Isaiah 66:23; Hebrews 4:9–11)

98. What is God's will for us in the fifth commandment?

That I honor, love, and be loyal to my father and mother and all those in authority over me; that I obey and submit to them, as is proper, when they correct and punish me; and also that I be patient with their failings— for through them God chooses to rule us.

(Exodus 21:17; Proverbs 1:8; 4:1; Romans 13:1, 2; Ephesians 5:21, 22; 6:1–9; Colossians 3:18–4:1; Proverbs 20:20; 23:22; 1 Peter 2:18; Matthew 22:21; Romans 13:1–8; Ephesians 6:1–9; Colossians 3:18–21)

99. What is God's will for us in the sixth commandment?

I am not to belittle, insult, hate, or kill my neighbor—not by my thoughts, my words, my look or gesture, and certainly not by actual deeds—and I am not to be party to this in others; rather, I am to put away all desire for revenge. I am not to harm or recklessly endanger myself either. Prevention of murder is also why government is armed with the sword.

(Genesis 9:6; Leviticus 19:17, 18; Matthew 5:21, 22; 26:52; Proverbs 25:21, 22; Matthew 18:35; Romans 18:35 Ephesians 4:26; Matthew 4:7; 26:52; Romans 13:11–14; Genesis 9:6; Exodus 21:14; Romans 13:4)

100. Does this commandment refer only to killing?

By forbidding murder God teaches us that He hates the root of murder: envy, hatred, anger, vindictiveness. In God's sight all such are murder.

(Proverbs 14:30; Romans 1:29; 12:19; Galatians 5:19–21; 1 John 2:9–11; 3:15)

101. Is it enough then that we do not kill our neighbor in any such way?

No. By condemning envy, hatred, and anger God tells us to love our neighbor as ourselves, to be patient, peace–loving, gentle, merciful, and friendly to him, to protect him from harm as much as we can, and to do good even to our enemies.

(Matthew 7:12; 22:39; Romans 12:10; Matthew 5:3–12; Luke 6:36; Romans 12:10, 18; Galatians 6:1, 2; Ephesians 4:2; Colossians 3:12; 1 Peter 3:8; Exodus 23:4, 5; Matthew 5:44, 45; Romans 12:20, 21 [Proverbs 25:21, 22])

102. What is God's will for us in the seventh commandment?

God condemns all unchastity. We should therefore thoroughly detest it and, married or single, live decent and chaste lives.

(Leviticus 18:30; Ephesians 5:3–5; Jude 22, 23; 1 Corinthians 7:1–9; 1 Thessalonians 4:3–8; Hebrews 13:4)

103. Does God, in this commandment, forbid only such scandalous sins as adultery?

We are temples of the Holy Spirit, body and soul, and God wants both to be kept clean and holy. That is why He forbids everything which incites unchastity, whether it be actions, look, talk, thoughts, or desires.

(1 Corinthians 15:33; Ephesians 5:18; Matthew 5:27–29; 1 Corinthians 6:18–20; Ephesians 5:3, 4)

104. What does God forbid in the eighth commandment?

He forbids not only outright theft and robbery, punishable by law. But in God's sight theft also includes cheating and swindling our neighbor by schemes made to appear legitimate, such as: inaccurate measurements of weight, size, or volume; fraudulent merchandising; counterfeit money; excessive interest; or any other means forbidden by God. In addition He forbids all greed and pointless squandering of His gifts.

(Exodus 22:1; 1 Corinthians 5:9, 10; 6:9, 10; Micah 6:9–11; Luke 3:14; James 5:1–6; Deuteronomy 25:13–16; Psalm 15:5; Proverbs 11:1; 12:22; Ezekiel 45:9–12; Luke 6:35; 12:15; Ephesians 5:5; Proverbs 21:20; 23:20, 21; Luke 16:10–13)

105. What does God require of you in this commandment?

That I do whatever I can for my neighbor's good, that I treat him as I would like others to treat me, and that I work faithfully so that I may share with those in need.

(Isaiah 58:5–10; Matthew 7:12; Galatians 6:9, 10; Ephesians 4:28)

106. What is God's will for us in the ninth commandment?

God's will is that I never give false testimony against anyone, twist no one's words, not gossip or slander, nor join in condemning anyone without a hearing or without a just cause. Rather, in court and everywhere else, I should avoid lying and deceit of every kind; these are devices the devil himself uses, and they would call down on me God's intense anger. I should love the truth, speak it candidly, and openly acknowledge it. And I should do what I can to guard and advance my neighbor's good name.

(Psalm 15; Proverbs 19:5; Matthew 7:1; Luke 6:37; Romans 1:28–32. Leviticus 19:11, 12; Proverbs 12:22; 13:5; John 8:44; Revelation 21:8; 1 Corinthians 13:6; Ephesians 4:25; 1 Peter 3:8, 9; 4:8)

107. What is God's will for us in the tenth commandment?

That not even the slightest thought or desire contrary to any one of God's commandments should ever arise in my heart. Rather, with all my heart I should always hate sin and take pleasure in whatever is right.

(Psalm 19:7–14; 139:23, 24; Romans 7:7, 8)

108. But can those converted to God obey these commandments perfectly?

No. In this life even the holiest have only a small beginning of this obedience. Nevertheless, with all seriousness of purpose, they do begin to live according to all, not only some, of God's commandments.

(Ecclesiastes 7:20; Romans 7:14, 15; 1 Corinthians 13:9; 1 John 1:8–10; Psalm 1:1, 2; Romans 7:22–25; Philippians 3:12–16)

109. No one in this life can obey the ten commandments perfectly: why then does God want them preached so pointedly?
First, so that the longer we live the more we may come to know our sinfulness and the more eagerly look to Christ for forgiveness of sins and righteousness. Second, so that, while praying to God for the grace of the Holy Spirit, we may never stop striving to be renewed more and more after God's image, until after this life we reach our goal: perfection.

(Psalm 32:5; Romans 3:19–26; 7:7, 24, 25; 1 John 1:9; 1 Corinthians 9:24; Philippians 3:12–14; 1 John 3:1–3)

110. Why do Christians need to pray?
Because prayer is the most important part of the thankfulness God requires of us. And also because God gives His grace and Holy Spirit only to those who pray continually and groan inwardly, asking God for these gifts and thanking Him for them.

(Psalm 50:14, 15; 116:12–19; 1 Thessalonians 5:16–18; Matthew 7:7, 8; Luke 11:9–13)

111. How does God want us to pray so that He will listen to us?

First, we must pray from the heart to no other than the one true God, who has revealed Himself in His Word, asking for everything He has commanded us to ask for. Second, we must acknowledge our need and misery, hiding nothing, and humble ourselves in His majestic presence. Third, we must rest on this unshakable foundation: even though we do not deserve it, God will surely listen to our prayer because of Christ our Lord. That is what He promised in His Word.

(Psalm 145:18–20; John 4:22–24; Romans 8:26, 27; James 1:5; 1 John 5:14, 15; 2 Chronicles 7:14; Psalm 2:11; 34:18; 62:8; Isaiah 66:2; Revelation 4; Daniel 9:17–19; Matthew 7:8; John 14:13, 14; 16:23; Romans 10:13; James 1:6)

112. What did God command us to pray for?

Everything we need, spiritually and physically, as embraced in the prayer Christ our Lord Himself taught us.

(James 1:17; Matthew 6:33)

113. What is this prayer?

Our Father in heaven, hallowed be Your name. Your kingdom come, Your will be done on earth as it is in heaven. Give us this day our daily bread. And forgive us our debts as we forgive our debtors. And do not lead us into temptation, but deliver us from the evil one. For Yours is the kingdom and the power and the glory forever. Amen.

(Matthew 6:9–13; Luke 11:2–4)

114. Why did Christ command us to call God, "our Father"?

At the very beginning of our prayer Christ wants to kindle in us what is basic to our prayer—the childlike awe and trust that God through Christ has become our Father. Our fathers do not refuse us the things of this life; God our Father will even less refuse to give us what we ask in faith.

(Matthew 7:9–11; Luke 11:11–13)

115. Why the words, "who art in heaven"?

These word teach us not to think of God's heavenly majesty as something earthly, and to expect everything for body and soul from His almighty power.

(Jeremiah 23:23, 24; Acts 17:24, 25; Matthew 6:25–34; Romans 8:31, 32)

116. What does the first request mean?

Hallowed be Your name means, help us to really know You, to bless, worship, and praise You for all Your works and for all that shines forth from them: Your almighty power, wisdom, kindness, justice, mercy, and truth. And it means, help us to direct all our living—what we think, say, and do—so that Your name will never be blasphemed because of us but always honored and praised.

(Jeremiah 9:23, 24; 31:33, 34; Matthew 16:17; John 17:3; Exodus 34:5–8; Psalm 145; Jeremiah 32:16–20; Luke 1:46–55, 68–75; Romans 11:33–36; Psalm 115:1; Matthew 5:16)

117. What does the second request mean?

Your kingdom come means, rule us by Your Word and Spirit in such a way that more and more we submit to You. Keep Your church strong, and add to it. Destroy the devil's work; destroy every force which revolts against You and every conspiracy against Your Word. Do this until Your kingdom is so complete and perfect that in it You are all in all.

(Matthew 7:21; 16:24–26; Luke 22:42; Romans 12:1, 2; Titus 2:11, 12; 1 Corinthians 7:17–24; Ephesians 6:5–9; Psalm 103:20, 21)

118. What does the fourth request mean?

Give us this day our daily bread means, do take care of all our physical needs so that we come to know that You are the only source of everything good, and that neither our work and worry nor Your gifts can do us any good without Your blessing. And so help us to give up our trust in creatures and to put trust in You alone.

(Psalm 104:27–30; 145:15, 16; Matthew 6:25–34; Acts 14:17; 17:25; James 1:17; Deuteronomy 8:3; Psalm 37:16; 127:1, 2; 1 Corinthians 15:58; Psalm 55:22; 62; 146; Jeremiah 17:5–8; Hebrews 13:5, 6)

119. What does the fifth request mean?

And forgive us our debts, as we also forgive our debtors means, because of Christ's blood, do not hold against us, poor sinners that we are, any of the sins we do or the evil that constantly clings to us. Forgive us just as we are fully determined, as evidence of Your grace in us, to forgive our neighbors.

(Psalm 51:1–7; 143:2; Romans 8:1; 1 John 2:1, 2; Matthew 6:14, 15; 18:21–35)

120. What does the sixth request mean?

And lead us not into temptation, but deliver us from evil means, by ourselves we are too weak to hold our own even for a moment. And our sworn enemies—the devil, the world, and our own flesh—never stop attacking us. And so, Lord, uphold us and make us strong with the strength of Your Holy Spirit, so that we may not go down to defeat in this spiritual struggle, but may firmly resist our enemies until we finally win the complete victory.

(Psalm 103:14–16; John 15:1–5; 2 Corinthians 11:14; Ephesians 6:10–13; 1 Peter 5:8; John 15:18–21; Romans 7:23; Galatians 5:17; Matthew 10:19, 20; 26:41; Mark 13:33; Romans 5:3–5; 1 Corinthians 10:13; 1 Thessalonians 3:13; 5:23)

121. What does your conclusion to this prayer mean?

For Yours is the kingdom, and the power, and the glory, forever means, we have made all these requests of You because, as our all-powerful King, You not only want to, but are able to give us all that is good; and because Your holy name, and not we ourselves, should receive all the praise, forever.

(Romans 10:11–13; 2 Peter 2:9; Psalm 115:1; John 14:13)

122. What does that little word "amen" mean?

Amen means, this is sure to be! It is even more sure that God listens to my prayer, than that I really desire what I pray for.

(Isaiah 65:24; 2 Corinthians 1:20; 2 Timothy 2:13)

66

The Scriptures of God are my only fountain and substance in all matters of weight and importance.

99

JOHN OWEN

66

The Bible in memory is better than the Bible in the book case.

99

C. H. SPURGEON

SCRIPTURE MEMORY

GALATIANS 2:20

I have been crucified with Christ. It is no longer I who live, but Christ who lives in me. And the life I now live in the flesh I live by faith in the Son of God, who loved me and gave himself for me.

JOHN 3:5–6

Jesus answered, "Truly, truly, I say to you, unless one is born of water and the Spirit, he cannot enter the kingdom of God. That which is born of the flesh is flesh, and that which is born of the Spirit is spirit."

PROVERBS 15:1–2

A soft answer turns away wrath,
but a harsh word stirs up anger.
The tongue of the wise commends knowledge,
but the mouths of fools pour out folly.

HEBREWS 12:14

Strive for peace with everyone, and for the holiness without which no one will see the Lord.

PSALM 46

God is our refuge and strength,
a very present help in trouble.
Therefore we will not fear though the earth gives way,
though the mountains be moved into the heart of the sea,
though its waters roar and foam,
though the mountains tremble at its swelling.

Selah

There is a river whose streams make glad the city of God,
the holy habitation of the Most High.
God is in the midst of her; she shall not be moved;
God will help her when morning dawns.
The nations rage, the kingdoms totter;
he utters his voice, the earth melts.
The Lord of hosts is with us;
the God of Jacob is our fortress.

Selah

Come, behold the works of the Lord,
how he has brought desolations on the earth.
He makes wars cease to the end of the earth;
he breaks the bow and shatters the spear;
he burns the chariots with fire.
"Be still, and know that I am God.
I will be exalted among the nations,
I will be exalted in the earth!"
The Lord of hosts is with us;
the God of Jacob is our fortress.

Selah

ROMANS 5:12–21

Therefore, just as sin came into the world through one man, and death through sin, and so death spread to all men because all sinned— for sin indeed was in the world before the law was given, but sin is not counted where there is no law. Yet death reigned from Adam to Moses, even over those whose sinning was not like the transgression of Adam, who was a type of the one who was to come.

But the free gift is not like the trespass. For if many died through one man's trespass, much more have the grace of God and the free gift by the grace of that one man Jesus Christ abounded for many. And the free gift is not like the result of that one man's sin. For the judgment following one trespass brought condemnation, but the free gift following many trespasses brought justification. For if, because of one man's trespass, death reigned through that one man, much more will those who receive the abundance of grace and the free gift of righteousness reign in life through the one man Jesus Christ.

Therefore, as one trespass led to condemnation for all men, so one act of righteousness leads to justification and life for all men. For as by the one man's disobedience the many were made sinners, so by the one man's obedience the many will be made righteous. Now the law came in to increase the trespass, but where sin increased, grace abounded all the more, so that, as sin reigned in death, grace also might reign through righteousness leading to eternal life through Jesus Christ our Lord.

PSALM 119:137–160

Tsadhe

Righteous are you, O Lord,
and right are your rules.
You have appointed your testimonies in
righteousness
and in all faithfulness.
My zeal consumes me,
because my foes forget your words.
Your promise is well tried,
and your servant loves it.
I am small and despised,
yet I do not forget your precepts.
Your righteousness is righteous forever,
and your law is true.
Trouble and anguish have found me out,
but your commandments are my delight.
Your testimonies are righteous forever;
give me understanding that I may live.

Qoph

With my whole heart I cry; answer me, O Lord!
I will keep your statutes.
I call to you; save me,
that I may observe your testimonies.
I rise before dawn and cry for help;
I hope in your words.
My eyes are awake before the watches of the night,
that I may meditate on your promise.
Hear my voice according to your steadfast love;
O Lord, according to your justice give me life.
They draw near who persecute me with evil purpose;

they are far from your law.
But you are near, O Lord,
and all your commandments are true.
Long have I known from your testimonies
that you have founded them forever.

Resh
Look on my affliction and deliver me,
for I do not forget your law.
Plead my cause and redeem me;
give me life according to your promise!
Salvation is far from the wicked,
for they do not seek your statutes.
Great is your mercy, O Lord;
give me life according to your rules.
Many are my persecutors and my adversaries,
but I do not swerve from your testimonies.
I look at the faithless with disgust,
because they do not keep your commands.
Consider how I love your precepts!
Give me life according to your steadfast love.
The sum of your word is truth,
and every one of your righteous rules
endures forever.

COLOSSIANS 1:12–17

Giving thanks to the Father, who has qualified you to share in the inheritance of the saints in light. He has delivered us from the domain of darkness and transferred us to the kingdom of his beloved Son, in whom we have redemption, the forgiveness of sins.

He is the image of the invisible God, the firstborn of all creation. For by him all things were created, in heaven and on earth, visible and invisible, whether thrones or dominions or rulers or authorities—all things were created through him and for him. And he is before all things, and in him all things hold together.

HEBREWS 12:1–2

Therefore, since we are surrounded by so great a cloud of witnesses, let us also lay aside every weight, and sin which clings so closely, and let us run with endurance the race that is set before us, looking to Jesus, the founder and perfecter of our faith, who for the joy that was set before him endured the cross, despising the shame, and is seated at the right hand of the throne of God.

ECCLESIASTES 12:1

Remember also your Creator in the days of your youth, before the evil days come and the years draw near of which you will say, "I have no pleasure in them"

JOSHUA 1:8

This Book of the Law shall not depart from your mouth, but you shall meditate on it day and night, so that you may be careful to do according to all that is written in it. For then you will make your way prosperous, and then you will have good success.

1 CORINTHIANS 10:31

So, whether you eat or drink, or whatever you do, do all to the glory of God.

ISAIAH 57:20–21

But the wicked are like the tossing sea;
for it cannot be quiet,
and its waters toss up mire and dirt.
There is no peace," says my God, "for the wicked."

1 JOHN 2:3–6

And by this we know that we have come to know him, if we keep his commandments. Whoever says "I know him" but does not keep his commandments is a liar, and the truth is not in him, but whoever keeps his word, in him truly the love of God is perfected. By this we may know that we are in him: whoever says he abides in him ought to walk in the same way in which he walked.

PSALM 119:161–176

Sin and Shin
   Princes persecute me without cause,
   but my heart stands in awe of your words.
   I rejoice at your word
   like one who finds great spoil.
   I hate and abhor falsehood,
   but I love your law.
   Seven times a day I praise you
   for your righteous rules.
   Great peace have those who love your law;
   nothing can make them stumble.

I hope for your salvation, O Lord,
and I do your commandments.
My soul keeps your testimonies;
I love them exceedingly.
I keep your precepts and testimonies,
for all my ways are before you.

Taw

Let my cry come before you, O Lord;
give me understanding according to your word!
Let my plea come before you;
deliver me according to your word.
My lips will pour forth praise,
for you teach me your statutes.
My tongue will sing of your word,
for all your commandments are right.
Let your hand be ready to help me,
for I have chosen your precepts.
I long for your salvation, O Lord,
and your law is my delight.
Let my soul live and praise you,
and let your rules help me.
I have gone astray like a lost sheep; seek your servant,
for I do not forget your commandments.

ROMANS 1:16–17

For I am not ashamed of the gospel, for it is the power of God for salvation to everyone who believes, to the Jew first and also to the Greek. For in it the righteousness of God is revealed from faith for faith, as it is written, "The righteous shall live by faith."

GALATIANS 6:14

But far be it from me to boast except in the cross of our Lord Jesus Christ, by which the world has been crucified to me, and I to the world.

JOHN 7:17

If anyone's will is to do God's will, he will know whether the teaching is from God or whether I am speaking on my own authority.

PROVERBS 16:16

How much better to get wisdom than gold!
To get understanding is to be chosen rather than silver.

PROVERBS 3:1–13

My son, do not forget my teaching,
but let your heart keep my commandments,
for length of days and years of life
and peace they will add to you.

Let not steadfast love and faithfulness forsake you;
bind them around your neck;
write them on the tablet of your heart.
So you will find favor and good success
in the sight of God and man.

Trust in the Lord with all your heart,
and do not lean on your own understanding.
In all your ways acknowledge him,
and he will make straight your paths.
Be not wise in your own eyes;
fear the Lord, and turn away from evil.
It will be healing to your flesh

and refreshment to your bones.

Honor the Lord with your wealth
and with the first-fruits of all your produce;
then your barns will be filled with plenty,
and your vats will be bursting with wine.

My son, do not despise the Lord's discipline
or be weary of his reproof,
for the Lord reproves him whom he loves,
as a father the son in whom he delights.

Blessed is the one who finds wisdom,
and the one who gets understanding,

1 CORINTHIANS 10:13

No temptation has overtaken you that is not
common to man. God is faithful, and he will not
let you be tempted beyond your ability, but with
the temptation he will also provide the way of
escape, that you may be able to endure it.

MATTHEW 25:31–40

When the Son of Man comes in his glory, and all
the angels with him, then he will sit on his glorious
throne. Before him will be gathered all the
nations, and he will separate people one from
another as a shepherd separates the sheep from
the goats. And he will place the sheep on his right,
but the goats on the left. Then the King will say to
those on his right, 'Come, you who are blessed by
my Father, inherit the kingdom prepared for you
from the foundation of the world. For I was

hungry and you gave me food, I was thirsty and you gave me drink, I was a stranger and you welcomed me, I was naked and you clothed me, I was sick and you visited me, I was in prison and you came to me.' Then the righteous will answer him, saying, 'Lord, when did we see you hungry and feed you, or thirsty and give you drink? And when did we see you a stranger and welcome you, or naked and clothe you? And when did we see you sick or in prison and visit you?' And the King will answer them, 'Truly, I say to you, as you did it to one of the least of these my brothers, you did it to me.'

COLOSSIANS 3:1–4

If then you have been raised with Christ, seek the things that are above, where Christ is, seated at the right hand of God. Set your minds on things that are above, not on things that are on earth. For you have died, and your life is hidden with Christ in God. When Christ who is your life appears, then you also will appear with him in glory.

ROMANS 12:1–2

I appeal to you therefore, brothers, by the mercies of God, to present your bodies as a living sacrifice, holy and acceptable to God, which is your spiritual worship. Do not be conformed to this world, but be transformed by the renewal of your mind, that by testing you may discern what is the will of God, what is good and acceptable and perfect.

PSALM 1

Blessed is the man
who walks not in the counsel of the wicked,
nor stands in the way of sinners,
nor sits in the seat of scoffers;
but his delight is in the law of the Lord,
and on his law he meditates day and night.

He is like a tree
planted by streams of water
that yields its fruit in its season,
and its leaf does not wither.
In all that he does, he prospers.
The wicked are not so,
but are like chaff that the wind drives away.

Therefore the wicked will not stand in the judgment,
nor sinners in the congregation of the righteous;
for the Lord knows the way of the righteous,
but the way of the wicked will perish.

PROVERBS 22:1

A good name is to be chosen rather than great riches,
and favor is better than silver or gold.

"

Always stand to it that your creed must bend
to the Bible, and not the Bible to your creed.

"

C. H. SPURGEON

"

Children are not a distraction from more important
work, they are the most important work.

"

C. S. LEWIS

BIBLE BASICS

THE TEN COMMANDMENTS
Summarized Version

1. You shall have no other gods before me.
2. You shall not make for yourself any carved image.
3. You shall not take the name of the LORD your God in vain.
4. Remember the Sabbath day, to keep it holy.
5. Honor your father and mother.
6. You shall not murder.
7. You shall not commit adultery.
8. You shall not steal.
9. You shall not bear false witness.
10. You shall not covet.

THE LORD'S PRAYER
Matthew 6:9-13

Pray then like this:
"Our Father in heaven,
hallowed be your name.
Your kingdom come,
your will be done,
on earth as it is in heaven.
Give us this day our daily bread,
and forgive us our debts,
as we also have forgiven our debtors.
And lead us not into temptation,
but deliver us from evil.

NAMES OF THE TWELVE APOSTLES
1. Simon Peter
2. Andrew
3. James (son of Zebedee)
4. John (son of Zebedee)
5. Philip
6. Bartholomew
7. Matthew
8. Thomas
9. James (son of Alphaeus)
10. Simon
11. Thaddaeus (Judas, son of James)
12. Judas Iscariot

THE APOSTLES' CREED

I believe in God, the Father Almighty,
the Maker of heaven and earth,
and in Jesus Christ, His only Son, our Lord:
Who was conceived by the Holy Ghost,
born of the virgin Mary,
suffered under Pontius Pilate,
was crucified, dead, and buried;
He descended into hell.
The third day He arose again from the dead;
He ascended into heaven,
and sitteth on the right hand of God the Father
Almighty;
from thence he shall come to judge the quick and
the dead.
I believe in the Holy Ghost;
the holy catholic church;
the communion of saints;
the forgiveness of sins;
the resurrection of the body;
and the life everlasting.
Amen.

(NOTE: The meaning of "catholic" is not to be
confused with the Roman Catholic Church. It
means universal.)

THE BOOKS OF THE BIBLE

Old Testament		
Genesis	II Chronicles	Daniel
Exodus	Ezra	Hosea
Leviticus	Nehemiah	Joel
Numbers	Esther	Amos
Deuteronomy	Job	Obadiah
Joshua	Psalm	Jonah
Judges	Proverbs	Micah
Ruth	Ecclesiastes	Nahum
I Samuel	Song of Solomon	Habakkuk
II Samuel	Isaiah	Zephaniah
I Kings	Jeremiah	Haggai
II Kings	Lamentations	Zechariah
I Chronicles	Ezekiel	Malachi

New Testament		
Matthew	Ephesians	Hebrews
Mark	Philippians	James
Luke	Colossians	I Peter
John	I Thessalonians	II Peter
Acts	II Thessalonians	I John
Romans	I Timothy	II John
I Corinthians	II Timothy	III John
II Corinthians	Titus	Jude
Galatians	Philemon	Revelation

THE NICENE CREED

I believe in one God, the Father Almighty, Maker of heaven and earth, and of all things visible and invisible.

And in one Lord Jesus Christ, the only-begotten Son of God, begotten of the Father before all worlds; God of God, Light of Light, very God of very God; begotten, not made, being of one substance with the Father, by whom all things were made.

Who, for us men and for our salvation, came down from heaven, and was incarnate by the Holy Spirit of the virgin Mary, and was made man; and was crucified also for us under Pontius Pilate; He suffered and was buried; and the third day He rose again, according to the Scriptures; and ascended into heaven, and sits on the right hand of the Father; and He shall come again, with glory, to judge the quick and the dead; whose kingdom shall have no end.

And I believe in the Holy Ghost, the Lord and Giver of Life; who proceeds from the Father and the Son; who with the Father and the Son together is worshipped and glorified; who spoke by the prophets.

And I believe in one holy catholic and apostolic Church. I acknowledge one baptism for the remission of sins; and I look for the resurrection of the dead, and the life of the world to come. Amen.

66

Beautiful music is the art of the prophets that can calm the agitations of the soul; it is one of the most magnificent and delightful presents God has given us.

99

MARTIN LUTHER

66

The foundation of worship in the heart is not emotional it is theological.

99

SINCLAIR FERGUSON

HYMNS

TO GOD BE THE GLORY
Words by Fanny Crosby (1875)

Verse 1

To God be the glory, great things He hath done;
So loved He the world that He gave us His Son,
Who yielded His life an atonement for sin,
And opened the lifegate that all may go in.

Refrain

Praise the Lord, praise the Lord,
Let the earth hear His voice!
Praise the Lord, praise the Lord,
Let the people rejoice!
O come to the Father, 'thro Jesus the Son,
And give Him the glory, great things He hath done.

Verse 2

O perfect redemption, the purchase of blood,
To ev'ry believer the promise of God;
The vilest offender who truly believes,
That moment from Jesus a pardon receives.

Refrain

Verse 3
Great things He hath taught us, great things He
hath done,
And great our rejoicing thro' Jesus the Son;
But purer, and higher, and greater will be
Our wonder, our transport, when Jesus we see.

Refrain

Amen.

COME BEHOLD THE WONDROUS MYSTERY

Words by Matt Boswell, Michael Bleecker, Matt Papa (2013)

Verse 1

Come behold the wondrous mystery
In the dawning of the King
He the theme of heaven's praises
Robed in frail humanity
In our longing, in our darkness
Now the light of life has come
Look to Christ, who condescended
Took on flesh to ransom us

Verse 2

Come behold the wondrous mystery
He the perfect Son of Man
In His living, in His suffering
Never trace nor stain of sin
See the true and better Adam
Come to save the hell-bound man
Christ the great and sure fulfillment
Of the law; in Him we stand

Verse 3

Come behold the wondrous mystery
Christ the Lord upon the tree
In the stead of ruined sinners
Hangs the Lamb in victory
See the price of our redemption

See the Father's plan unfold
Bringing many sons to glory
Grace unmeasured, love untold

Verse 4
Come behold the wondrous mystery
Slain by death the God of life
But no grave could e'er restrain Him
Praise the Lord; He is alive!
What a foretaste of deliverance
How unwavering our hope
Christ in power resurrected
As we will be when he comes
What a foretaste of deliverance
How unwavering our hope
Christ in power resurrected
As we will be when he comes

AND CAN IT BE THAT I SHOULD GAIN?
Words by Charles Wesley (1738)

Verse 1

And can it be that I should gain
An int'rest in the Savior's blood?
Died He for me, who caused His pain?
For me, who Him to death pursued?
Amazing love! How can it be
That Thou, my God, shouldst die for me?

Refrain

Amazing love! How can it be
That Thou, my God, shouldst die for me?

Verse 2

'Tis mystery all, th' Immortal dies:
Who can explore this strange design?
In vain the first born seraph tries
To sound the depth of love divine.
'Tis mercy all! Let earth adore,
Let angel minds inquire no more.

Refrain

Verse 3

He left His Father's throne above,
So free, so infinite His grace;
Emptied Himself of all but love,
And bled for Adam's helpless race.
'Tis mercy all! Immense and free!
For, O my God, it found out me.

Refrain

Verse 4
Long my imprisoned spirit lay
Fast bound in sin and nature's night;
Thine eye diffused a quick'ning ray;
I woke, the dungeon flamed with light!
My chains fell off; my heart was free;
I rose, went forth and followed Thee.

Refrain

Verse 5
No condemnation now I dread;
Jesus, and all in Him, is mine!
Alive in Him, my living Head,
And clothed in righteousness divine,
Bold I approach th' eternal throne,
And claim the crown through Christ my own.

Refrain

FACING A TASK UNFINISHED

Words by Frank Houghton (1931) and Keith & Kristyn Getty

Verse 1

Facing a task unfinished
That drives us to our knees
A need that, undiminished
Rebukes our slothful ease
We, who rejoice to know Thee
Renew before Thy throne
The solemn pledge we owe Thee
To go and make Thee known

Verse 2

Where other lords beside Thee
Hold their unhindered sway
Where forces that defied Thee
Defy Thee still today
With none to heed their crying
For life, and love, and light
Unnumbered souls are dying
And pass into the night

Refrain

We go to all the world
With kingdom hope unfurled
No other name has power to save
But Jesus Christ The Lord

Verse 4

We bear the torch that flaming

Fell from the hands of those
Who gave their lives proclaiming
That Jesus died and rose
Ours is the same commission
The same glad message ours
Fired by the same ambition
To Thee we yield our powers

Refrain

Verse 5
O Father who sustained them
O Spirit who inspired
Saviour, whose love constrained them
To toil with zeal untired
From cowardice defend us
From lethargy awake!
Forth on Thine errands send us
To labour for Thy sake

Refrain

ALL PEOPLE THAT ON EARTH DO DWELL
Words by William Kethe (1561) from
Psalm 100

Verse 1

All people that on earth do dwell,
Sing to the Lord with cheerful voice;
Him serve with fear, His praise forthtell,
Come ye before Him and rejoice.

Verse 2

The Lord ye know is God indeed;
Without our aid He did us make;
We are His folk, He doth us feed,
And for His sheep He doth us take.

Verse 3

O enter then His gates with praise,
Approach with joy His courts unto;
Praise, laud and bless His name always,
For it is seemly so to do.

Verse 4

For why? The Lord our God is good,
His mercy is forever sure;
His truth at all times firmly stood,
And shall from age to age endure.

Amen.

GREAT GOD OF WONDERS!

Words by Samuel Davies (1769)

Verse 1

Great God of wonders! All Thy ways
Are matchless, Godlike, and divine;
But the fair glories of Thy grace
More Godlike and unrivaled shine,
More Godlike and unrivaled shine.

Refrain

Who is a pard'ning God like Thee?
Or who has grace so rich and free?
Or who has grace so rich and free?

Verse 2

In wonder lost, with trembling joy,
We take the pardon of our God:
Pardon for crimes of deepest dye,
A pardon bought with Jesus' blood,
A pardon bought with Jesus' blood.

Refrain

Verse 3

O may this strange, this matchless grace,
This Godlike miracle of love,
Fill the whole earth with grateful praise,
And all th' angelic choirs above,
And all th' angelic choirs above.

Refrain

HOW SAD OUR STATE BY NATURE IS!

Words by Isaac Watts (1707)

Verse 1

How sad our state by nature is!
Our sin, how deep it stains!
And Satan binds our captive minds,
Fast in his slavish chains.

Verse 2

But there's a voice of sovereign grace,
Sounds from the sacred word;
"Ho! Ye despairing sinners, come,
And trust upon the Lord."

Verse 3

My soul obeys th' almighty call,
And runs to this relief;
I would believe thy promise, Lord;
Oh! Help my unbelief.

Verse 4

To the dear fountain of Thy blood,
Incarnate God, I fly;
Here let me wash my spotted soul
From crimes of deepest dye.

Verse 5

Stretch out Thine arm, victorious King,
My reigning sins subdue;
Drive the old Dragon from his seat,
With all his hellish crew.

Verse 6
A guilty, weak, and helpless worm,
On Thy kind arms I fall:
Be Thou my strength and righteousness,
My Jesus and My All.

NOT WHAT MY HANDS HAVE DONE
Words by Horatius Bonar (1864)

Verse 1

Not what my hands have done,
Can save my guilty soul;
Not what my toiling flesh has borne
Can make my spirit whole.
Not what I feel or do
Can give me peace with God;
Not all my prayers and sighs and tears
Can bear my awful load.

Verse 2

Thy work alone, O Christ,
Can ease this weight of sin;
Thy blood alone, O Lamb of God,
Can give me peace within.
Thy love to me, O God,
Not mine, O Lord, to Thee,
Can rid me of this dark unrest
And set my spirit free.

Verse 3

Thy grace alone, O God,
To me can pardon speak;
Thy power alone, O Son of God,
Can this sore bondage break.
No other work, save Thine,
No other blood will do;
No strength, save that which is divine,
Can bear me safely through.

Verse 4

I bless the Christ of God;
I rest on love divine;
And with unfalt'ring lip and heart,
I call this Savior mine.
His cross dispels each doubt;
I bury in His tomb
Each thought of unbelief and fear,
Each ling'ring shade of gloom.

Verse 5

I praise the God of grace,
I trust His truth and might;
He calls me His, I call Him mine,
My God, my joy, my light.
'Tis He who saveth me,
And freely pardon gives;
I love because He loveth me,
I live because He lives.

66

The word of God can be in the mind without being in the heart, but it cannot be in the heart without first being in the mind.

99

R. C. SPROUL

66

You may speak but a word to a child, and in that child there may be slumbering a noble heart which shall stir the Christian Church in years to come.

99

C. H. SPURGEON

TRACK YOUR PROGRESS

The following is a suggested guide from Book 3 divided into suggested age with a column to record the date of mastery. If you are not beginning with age fourteen, we suggest that you begin with the recommended scripture, hymns, etc. for your child by age as well as with question #1 of the *Heidelberg Catechism: A Baptist Version*. The catechism is written in a systematic format with each question built upon those before it. The memorization of the whole catechism will expose the child to a solid doctrinal foundation.

AGE FOURTEEN

Heidelberg Catechism: A Baptist Version

Questions #1-5	Date: _____
Questions #6-10	Date: _____
Questions #11-15	Date: _____
Questions #16-19	Date: _____

Scriptures

Galatians 2:20	Date: _____
John 3:5–6	Date: _____
Proverbs 15:1–2	Date: _____
Hebrews 12:14	Date: _____
Psalm 46	Date: _____
Romans 5:12–21	Date: _____
Psalm 119:137–160	Date: _____

Bible Basics

The Ten Commandments	Date: _____
The Lord's Prayer	Date: _____

Hymns

To God Be the Glory	Date: _____
Come Behold the Wondrous Mystery	Date: _____

AGE FIFTEEN

Heidelberg Catechism: A Baptist Version

Questions #20-24	Date: _____
Questions #25-29	Date: _____
Questions #30-34	Date: _____
Questions #35-39	Date: _____
Questions #40-44	Date: _____
Questions #45-51	Date: _____

Scriptures

Colossians 1:12–17	Date: _____
Hebrews 12:1–2	Date: _____
Ecclesiastes 12:1	Date: _____
Joshua 1:8	Date: _____
1 Corinthians 10:31	Date: _____
Isaiah 57:20–21	Date: _____
1 John 2:3–6	Date: _____
Psalm 119: 161–176	Date: _____

Bible Basics

The Names of the Twelve Apostles	Date: _____
The Apostles' Creed	Date: _____

Hymns

And Can It Be That I Should Gain?	Date: _____
Facing a Task Unfinished	Date: _____

AGE SIXTEEN

Heidelberg Catechism: A Baptist Version

Questions #52-57   Date: _____
Questions #58-63   Date: _____
Questions #64-69   Date: _____
Questions #70-74   Date: _____
Questions #75-79   Date: _____
Questions #80-85   Date: _____

Scriptures

Romans 1:16–17   Date: _____
Galatians 6:14   Date: _____
John 7:17   Date: _____
Proverbs 16:16   Date: _____
Proverbs 3:1–13   Date: _____
1 Corinthians 10:13   Date: _____

Bible Basics

The Books of the Bible   Date: _____

Hymns

All People that
on Earth Do Dwell   Date: _____
Great God of Wonders!   Date: _____

AGE SEVENTEEN

Heidelberg Catechism: A Baptist Version

Questions #86-90	Date: _____
Questions #91-95	Date: _____
Questions #96-100	Date: _____
Questions #101-105	Date: _____
Questions #106-110	Date: _____
Questions #111-115	Date: _____
Questions #116-122	Date: _____

Scriptures

Matthew 25:31–40	Date: _____
Colossians 3:1–4	Date: _____
Romans 12:1–2	Date: _____
Psalm 1	Date: _____
Proverbs 22:1	Date: _____

Bible Basics

The Nicene Creed	Date: _____

Hymns

How Sad Our State by Nature Is	Date: _____
Not What My Hands Have Done	Date: _____